Santa's
REINDEER
STICKER ACTIVITY BOOK

Have fun completing the sticker and doodling activities! Look at the sticker sheets. Can you find a sticker that fits? When you are sure you have found the right sticker, carefully peel it off and stick it down. There are also cute press-outs and extra stickers to use anywhere you want!

make believe ideas

Festive fun

Find the missing stickers, then follow the lines to see which chimney Santa visits.

Circle five differences between the scenes.

Colourful cards

Colour and sticker the cards.

Snappy Christmas!

Sweet pairs

Find the missing stickers, then draw lines to match the pairs.

Sticker more sweets in the jars.

Toy shopping

Find the missing stickers
to fill the shelves.

Sticker the trucks, then circle
the one that is different.

Colour the
cuddly elephant.

Silly snowman

Use colour and stickers to finish the snowman.

Ho, ho, ho!

Colour the reindeer's home.

Find the missing stickers
and decorate the stockings.

Christmas-tree challenge

Find the missing sticker, then help the car through the maze to find the tree sale.

Start

SALE

Finish

Sticker the cars, then circle the two that match.

Use colour and stickers to finish the tree.

9

Present surprise

Finish the present, then follow the lines to see who it belongs to.

Sticker and trace the numbers to finish the sums.

six

3 + 3 = ●

four

● **+ 2 = 4**

Christmas pattern

Use stickers to finish the pattern.

Trace the dots to copy Mrs Claus, then add colour.

Sticker the missing holly.

Santa's sleigh ride

Use colour and stickers to finish the scene.

Sticker the robins, then circle the one that doesn't match.

14

Colour the festive pattern.

Holiday bakes

Colour the Christmas food.

Trace the pattern, then colour the cookie tin.

Christmas party

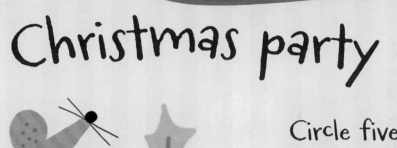

Circle five differences between the scenes.

Use stickers to finish the pattern.